101

HORSEKEEPING TIPS

Other books in the series

101 Simple Strategies for a Safer and More Efficient Stable
HORSEKEEPING TIPS

Jessie Shiers

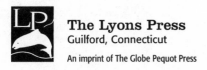

The Lyons Press
Guilford, Connecticut
An imprint of The Globe Pequot Press

Copyright © 2005 by Morris Book Publishing, LLC

The Lyons Press is an imprint of The Globe Pequot Press

10 9 8 7 6 5 4 3 2

Printed in the United States of America

Designed by Sheryl P. Kober

ISBN-13: 978-1-59228-831-1
ISBN-10: 1-59228-831-6

Library of Congress Cataloging-in-Publication Data

Shiers, Jessie.
  101 horsekeeping tips : simple strategies for a safer and more efficient stable / Jessie Shiers.
     p. cm.
  ISBN 1-59228-831-6 (trade paper)
  1. Horses. 2. Horses—Feeding and feeds. 3. Horses—Health. 4. Stables—Management. I. Title. II. Title: One hundred one horsekeeping tips.
SF285.3.S54 2005
636.1'083—dc22

                                                                2005021540

Contents

Introduction

Accepting the privilege of horse ownership begins with understanding that we are taking on an enormous responsibility. Our horses are our friends, companions, partners, teammates, and soul mates. They give us so much, so willingly—their strength, stamina, agility, and beauty—to give us the chance to vicariously experience the freedom and power that comes so naturally to them. Because we keep our horses locked in boxes or fenced in paddocks, we have taken away their ability to care for themselves as they do in the wild, roaming in search of food and water. They depend on us for their every need and desire. Therefore, we as horse owners carry a solemn responsibility to provide the best possible lives for our equine partners.

A horse's minimum requirements are water and food, a clean, sheltered place to sleep, and exercise. The hallmarks of any well-run stable are cleanliness, safety, and efficiency. The health and happiness of the horses are the barn owner and manager's paramount concerns. To meet these needs does not need to cost a lot of money, and can be done at all levels—large, elaborate stables and backyard barns alike can provide horses with excellent care. All it takes is dedication and attention to detail.

Within these pages you'll find useful information and good ideas to help you meet these needs in ways that don't compromise your wallet or your schedule. In "Feed and Nutrition," you'll learn, among other things, how to tell whether your horse is getting too much protein in his grain or not enough carotene in his hay. In the section on "Health," you'll find tips for spotting and preventing minor health problems before they become major ones. Under the "Safety" net, you'll find out what can be dangerous about a winter blanket, and you'll learn the correct method for freeing a cast horse.

In this little book, there's a little innovation, a little traditional wisdom, and a lot of common sense. Along the way, keep in mind the most important tip of all: "Have a great ride!"

Care, and not fine stables,

makes a **good horse**.

—Danish proverb

tip 1. Before building or making any major changes to your facility, it's wise to learn about local regulations. Your local planning and zoning office can provide information on such matters as how many animals are allowed per acre; where manure piles and outbuildings should be located in relation to wells, neighboring properties, roads, and wetlands; whether you may build new structures on your land; snow-weight ratings for roofs; and how to determine where power and gas lines are before you begin digging.

This horse enjoys the shade provided by a clean, dry, spacious run-in shed. (photos.com)

tip 2.

When constructing a run-in shed, take into consideration the wind and sun patterns for your area, the lay of the land, and the number of horses that will be using the shed. In most areas, a shed facing south will provide the best protection from wind and the greatest exposure to the sun in the wintertime. Since the shed will be experiencing quite a bit of horse traffic and is likely to fill up with manure, build it on a high spot with good drainage. However, it should also be located close to your barn or house so that you can monitor the horses and conveniently clean it out on a regular basis.

Finally, recognize that the horses will have to share the run-in, and many horses can be quite territorial. Be sure to provide for an area of at least 12 feet by 12 feet for each horse. Despite this generous space allowance, territorial disputes may occur, so check on your horses regularly in bad weather to be sure all horses are being allowed to use the shed.

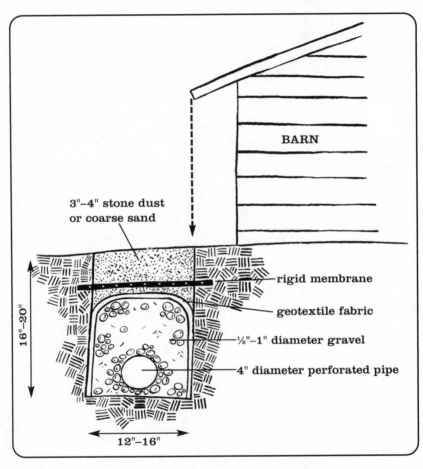

A French drain diverts water from around the sides of buildings without being an eyesore.

tip 3.

Prevent the flooding of stables and riding rings by planning drainage well. If you're constructing a new facility, think through the drainage question well before choosing your site. If necessary, consult with a professional contractor. Bad drainage can utterly ruin otherwise excellent facilities during the wet season. If your barn or arena has already been built and is experiencing regular flooding and erosion, a trench (or *swale*) dug around the higher side is a relatively simple fix to divert water that causes flooding and erosion. A more complex and costly solution, but one that is ultimately more attractive and effective, is to construct French drains underground.

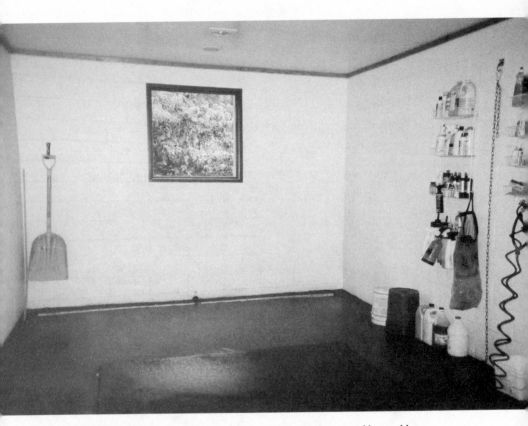

The floor of this wash stall is made of brushed concrete covered by a rubber mat. (Courtesy of Caroline Dowd)

tip 4.

All barn aisles should have non-slip footing, both for human and equine safety. When considering footing choices, think about whether the material will be slippery if it becomes wet (which it inevitably will). Some common, safe aisle footing choices are:

- Textured concrete, made by brushing or raking the fresh concrete before it sets. This is one of the most durable, least expensive options.

- Packed dirt, which generally has good traction unless it has a high percentage of clay, in which case it can be surprisingly slippery when wet. Although a dirt floor may seem like the ultimate in frugality, it can be difficult to maintain, as hooves, rakes, and other routine traffic wear it away, causing ruts and uneven spots.

- Rubber mats, which are the ideal option in terms of safety, ease of cleaning, attractiveness, and durability; however, they are also quite expensive.

This Appaloosa seems sensible enough. But if he tries to reach for grass on the far side of the barbed wire fence, he'll lacerate his face and neck on the rusty barbs. (photos.com)

tip 5.

Do not use barbed wire for horse fencing. A horse that becomes entangled in the wire will panic and struggle, injuring himself badly on the barbs. Aggressive horses will sometimes drive a less dominant horse through a fence, or panicked horses may stampede and attempt to escape from a pasture. In such cases, barbed wire fencing is unlikely to break, but will trap the already frightened horse or horses and cause lacerations. Play it safe and use a fencing material that is designed for horses, such as wood, PVC, steel panels, or electrical tape.

This PVC fencing is costly but makes an attractive and safe perimeter fence.

tip 6. Good fencing is one of the most impor-

tant investments to consider as you develop your horse property. While high-quality fencing can be quite expensive, this is not the place to skimp. Poor fencing invites accidents, as horses can escape and run into trouble on neighboring farms or, even worse, on roads. Especially in suburban stables on small acreage, it's a wise idea to line your entire property with a sturdy, visually appealing fence such as painted wood or PVC fencing. Horses that do escape either from their stalls or from interior paddocks will still be safely contained on your own property. Interior fences can then be safely constructed of less expensive materials, such as electrical tape.

This large compost pile is turned with a tractor. Once a year, a local landscaping company buys it and hauls it away. (Jason Shiers)

tip 7. For the horse owner with just two or

three horses, composting can be an ideal answer to the manure question. The benefits are many: the internal heat generated by a compost heap kills parasites and fly eggs, resulting in lowered risk of parasite infestation in your horses and—of course—fewer flies. A well-maintained compost heap is virtually odorless, and its volume will decrease by about 50 percent. The resulting product will be a useful and valuable soil additive for your garden or your hayfields. Your friends, neighbors, and local greenhouses may actually *want* to take your composted manure!

Start by building piles of manure and bedding. Each pile will need to be at least 1 cubic yard in size. Ideally, you'll want to build several covered bins for your composting system. To avoid creating pollution, locate your compost piles at least 50 feet from ponds and streams and 100 feet from drinking-water wells. Check local regulations for exact limits.

Turn the piles occasionally with a pitchfork to help maintain oxygen levels, distribute moisture, and keep the microorganisms working. The piles will generate quite a bit of internal heat from the decomposition—up to 120 degrees Fahrenheit; you'll know it's time to turn the pile when it starts cooling down. The compost pile is finished and ready to be used as fertilizer when it stays cool even after you've turned it, the volume is reduced by half, and it looks like soil.

Although Jim lives with two other horses, he prefers the company of this steer. (Kim Peterson)

tip 8.
An old saying goes, "To a horseman, one of the saddest sights is a field with one horse." Horses are herd animals, and they will not be happy when kept alone. If you don't want to take on the cost of buying, feeding, and stabling another mature, rideable horse, consider several options. One is to take in an elderly, retired pony or even a miniature. Smaller equines require less feed and bedding, typically go barefoot (although they will still need regular trimming by a farrier), and require less maintenance overall. Another option is to keep different kinds of livestock. Horses have been known to befriend goats, cattle, and even pigs. Goats are common horse companions, but if you plan to keep one, take into consideration its special fencing needs. Goats are notorious escape artists with a tremendous ability to leap tall fences in a single bound (see tip 90 for a photo of good goat fencing).

Cows can help contribute to the health of the pasture, because while horses will eat young, tender grass shoots, cows prefer the mature plants and weeds that horses reject. Pasturing horses and cattle in the same field thus results in a balanced pasture.

George is learning how to canter down a snow-covered hill without slipping. (Jason Shiers)

tip 9.

Much of the work we do with our horses is on flat, level, consistent footing. Although good and safe, it doesn't allow for a complete physical development of the horse. If it's at all possible, try to turn your horses out on hilly, uneven terrain. The hills will help develop the musculature of their backs, stifles, and hindquarters as they run and play, and even as they stroll casually up and down in search of a better patch of grass. Uneven, irregular footing also helps to develop agility, surefootedness, and balance.

Young horses benefit from this exercise in preparation for their under-saddle training: they will be stronger and better balanced than horses of the same age who grew up in flat paddocks. Mature horses are able to keep themselves fit and healthy. Older, retired horses stay healthy and sound longer when they are able to exercise on hills.

Jim enjoys the shade provided by these trees on a hot day, but they may be in danger if he decides that the bark is tasty.

tip 10. For those of us lucky enough to

have a few large, non-poisonous trees in a pasture, they are a great asset, providing shade from the sun and shelter from rain and wind. When the grass gets a bit low or your horses are extra curious, they may begin to nibble at the bark of the trees and can quickly kill an entire tree by *girdling* it—chewing off the bark all the way around the trunk. Bark carries nutrients to and from the leaves and roots, so when it is removed, the tree dies and becomes an eyesore as well as a hazard when branches begin to rot and fall off. Protect trees in your turnout area by wrapping them with chicken wire from the base up to about 6 feet. Cover the sharp edges of the wire with heavy tape to prevent horses from cutting themselves.

A **cowman** saddles and un-saddles his own horse, and an offer to help is **unwelcome.**

—Ramon Adams,
The Cowman's Code of Ethics

tip 11.

So you've washed your white saddle pads three times, bleached them twice, and they're still dingy-looking? Here's how to get them gleaming again: Instead of bleach or laundry detergent, use the blue horse shampoo that's designed for gray horses (such as Quiksilver). Squeeze a little onto the extra-dirty spots around the withers and under the girth area and scrub it in. Add a bit more shampoo to the washing machine as it's filling with water. Then toss in your filthy pads, and in twenty minutes they'll be as good as new.

tip 12. Many under-saddle problems are

caused by back pain associated with poor saddle fit. To find out whether your horse's back is aching, palpate the long, thin muscles on either side of his spine with your thumbs and fingertips, starting at the withers and working your way toward his croup. You should be able to press fairly hard without getting a reaction. Also try raking your fingernails down each side of his back, again from the withers toward the tail. If the horse throws his head, moves away, pins his ears, or tries to bite or kick, it can indicate bad saddle fit or even an injury such as a pulled muscle. Try to identify the most reactive spots and use that knowledge as you evaluate your saddle's fit. It may need different padding or it may need to be *reflocked* (restuffed by a professional saddler), or you may just need a different saddle. In some cases, back pain can be a symptom of a problem elsewhere, such as arthritic hocks.

George's blanket will go to the cleaners as soon as it is warm enough to stop using it.

tip 13.

Take your blankets to a cleaner as soon as the weather warms up in the spring. Leaving them sitting around all summer will allow bacteria to breed in the moist folds, supported by the caked-on manure. In addition to the foul smell, sweat and mud will degrade the materials and rot the stitching. Cleaning blankets immediately and storing them in a cool, dry place will extend their life. What's more, if you wait until next fall to have the blankets cleaned, most cleaners will be overwhelmed and won't be able to return your blankets to you by the time you need them, and they may charge an extra fee for the rush.

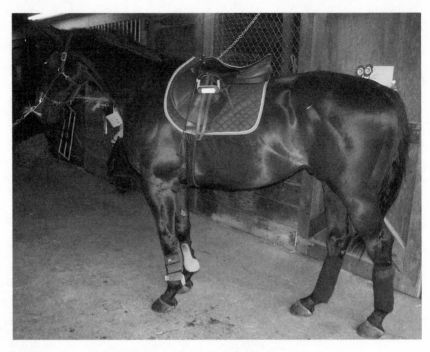

George's saddle, girth, and leg wraps show the benefits of good daily care. (Jason Shiers)

tip 14.

To keep leather tack soft, supple, and safe, clean it often and store it in a cool, dry place away from feed that can attract rodents. Keep your saddle covered with a saddle cover or even just a towel to keep dust off it. Don't toss your sweaty saddle pad on top of the saddle after a ride. Either allow the saddle pad to dry in the sun, or launder it immediately. Hose off sweaty or muddy horse boots and let them air dry before storing. The girth, bridle, and any other leather that comes into direct contact with the horse's body should be cleaned with glycerine saddle soap and lukewarm water after every ride. This extra effort will remove sweat and grime that dry the leather, degrade the stitching, and host bacteria and fungus that will be transferred to your horse the next time you use the tack.

tip 15.

In some stables, grooms and so-called trainers use a technique called *earing*, in which the horse's ear is grabbed and twisted, to force a horse to stand still. The function is somewhat like the action of a nose twitch, but it is very painful and severe. Horses who have been eared can be difficult to bridle because they are terrified of having their ears touched.

Judy Richter, a noted hunter/jumper trainer at Coker Farm in Bedford, New York, explains her method for bridling an ear-shy horse or pony: "A pony that has been abused in his earlier life will need extra time and patience. If you find you have to deal with such a creature, unhook the bridle on the left side—cheek piece and noseband. With one hand, offer him a carrot; with the other, slip the headstall quietly over his ears. Then slip the bit into his mouth and hook up the cheek piece and noseband. Coaxing gets it done. Temper and beating do not."

Aside from horses that have been eared, Judy mentions that some horses are ear-shy because they "have eczema in their ears that never bothers them except when someone tries to touch or treat it. Because it is basically harmless, most vets recommend the condition be left alone."

We attended stables, as we attended church, in our best clothes, no doubt showing the degree of respect due to horses, no less than to **the deity.**

—Sir Osbert Sitwell,
The Scarlet Tree

George walks willingly toward me in the pasture, knowing that a treat is in store. (Jason Shiers)

tip 16.

If your pasture-kept horses are only caught for veterinary or farrier care or to be worked, then of course they may become hard to catch. They are smart! But for safety and convenience, all horses should be trained to come willingly whenever you want them. If your horses have developed the vice of running away when they see you approaching with a lead rope, make a point of catching them frequently for no reason other than to give them a pat and a treat. Or if a certain horse enjoys being groomed, for example, then bring him in occasionally just for a friendly grooming session. Give him a carrot, and send him back out to join the herd.

You can avoid hard-to-catch behavior altogether by rewarding your horse each time he lets you catch him easily. Every time I greet my horse, even when he's in his stall, I give him a bit of carrot. Now when I walk out into the pasture for him, he anticipates this gift and comes right up to me.

Venturing into a field full of horses with a bucket of grain can result in a dangerous feeding frenzy with you at its center. Rather than bribing your horse by shaking a grain bucket or waving a carrot, pocket a small piece of carrot that you can surreptitiously slip to him as a reward without any of the other horses noticing. This way, you won't have to fight through the hungry herd to find your horse, yet over time he will learn that Mom walking toward him with a lead rope means snacks are coming.

tip 17.

A relatively recent innovation in the ongoing war against flies are fly predators. There are two kinds: nematodes (microscopic worms) and fly parasites (tiny, nonstinging relatives of the wasp). Fly predators, which can be bought through the mail, arrive in paper bags. When you release them around your stable, the nematodes burrow in the soil and release a bacteria that kills fly larvae, on which they then feed. The bacteria is harmless to humans, horses, and other animals. The fly parasite wasps find fly pupae and destroy them by laying their own eggs inside them. The fly parasites do not bite, sting, or swarm, and they are nocturnal and so tiny—about the size of gnats—that you will never notice them.

tip 18.
Cobwebs, a common sight around the corners of many barns, are not only unsightly, but they can be a fire hazard. A spark or lightning strike at one corner of a stable can quickly blaze through the entire barn by traveling along the cobwebs. While barn fires are not common, they are devastating when they do occur. Reduce the risk by regularly sweeping out cobwebs. Duct tape your broom to a long pole to reach the rafters. If you use a vacuum cleaner for cobwebs, tape a long PVC pipe to the end of the vacuum cleaner hose to extend its reach.

Bonus tip: In order to slow down the growth of cobwebs, try this simple solution at the beginning of each summer. After thoroughly sweeping out all webs, rinse down the walls with a mild solution of water and household antiseptic such as Lysol. The chemical will discourage spiders from setting up housekeeping in your stable.

---

tip 19.

Horses who are bored or have too much energy often develop stable vices. After cribbing, one of the most annoying, destructive, and tenacious habits is stall-walking. Stall-walkers pace in endless small circles in their stalls, making a racket that is distracting to anyone trying to work in the barn. They bore holes in their stall floors, even wearing through thick rubber mats in a matter of weeks. They stir up the bedding, making the stall messy and difficult to clean. They put great strain on their ligaments and joints. And they are impossible to keep in good weight.

The first course of action, Judy Richter counsels, is turnout. "Turning such horses out on grass, or else making sure they always have a little hay to nibble on in the barn to keep them occupied, can make a difference." If these tactics fail, another choice is to place obstacles that make it more difficult for him to walk around in the stall, and may also provide some entertainment. Judy says that "several tires randomly placed in the stall-walker's stall will discourage him from pacing round and round." Alternatively, try hanging several safe objects from the ceiling with baling twine. Commercially made horse play balls or treat holders work well, or you could just use empty gallon milk jugs.

Pasture rotation helps preserve grass. (Jason Shiers)

tip 20. If you have the acreage to do it,

advises Mott Atherholt of Red Fox Farm in Virginia, "practice pasture rotation." She recommends grazing horses for three weeks in a pasture and then letting it stand unused for one week. "During the week the pasture is open," Mott continues, "harrow the pasture to break up manure. The rotation and harrowing will help curb the development of parasites," and will allow the grass to regrow.

Even if your available pasture is very small—less than one acre per horse—rotation can help preserve some of the grass, especially if you create a *sacrifice area* (see tip 48) and only allow the horses to be on grass for a few hours per day and supplement their diets with hay.

tip 21.

Caroline Dowd, a top eventing rider and trainer at Quarter Run Farm in Carthage, North Carolina, must keep track of many horses and people in her busy training stable. To make sure that she can contact the right people quickly in case of an emergency, she posts important phone numbers in a prominent place in the barn. "This list should include each horse's vet, farrier, and owner's number, plus a backup person to call if the owner is not available," she advises. If a particular horse is insured, she includes the name of the insurance company and the policy number. Lists may either be posted individually beside each horse's stall door, or may be combined into one list beside the barn phone. "This list must be kept up to date," Caroline stresses.

tip 22. Professional instructors, trainers,

and stable owners should provide a price list for boarders and stu-
dents. List each service and its cost. This will both discourage misunderstandings ("What? You're charging me *how much* for wrapping
my horse's injured leg??") and possibly encourage clients to request
services that they may not otherwise have known about. A trainer's
or instructor's price list would include fees for hour, half-hour, private,
semi-private, and group lessons; travel expenses for training or
coaching at a show; showing a horse in a class; half-hour or one-hour
training rides; accompanying you on a trail ride; per-mile rates for
shipping; and commission fees associated with the purchase or sale
of a horse.

A stable owner's price list for boarders may be much more exten-
sive and will include some or all of the following: basic cost of full,
rough, pasture, or training board; mane pulling; bathing; sheath
cleaning; braiding; clipping; grooming; tacking/untacking; cooling
out; blanketing; lunging; extra turnout or private turnout; tack cleaning; and medical care including cold-hosing, poulticing, wrapping,
hand-walking, administering oral, intravenous, or intramuscular medications, and assisting the vet, dentist, or farrier.

Signage that clearly indicates the rules helps keep a stable running smoothly. (photos.com)

tip 23. Any barn that has boarders should

post a list of barn rules. This list will prevent misunderstandings that can lead to tension between management and clients. Such a list would include barn hours, feeding and turnout restrictions, clean-up expectations, riding arena etiquette, requirements for wearing riding helmets, restricted areas (such as equipment sheds), safety rules regarding children and dogs, speed limits for vehicles and horses, and smoking regulations. Keep the list updated as new situations arise. For example, certain pastures may be restricted for grazing and riding in the spring to allow the grass to grow, while in the winter the wash stall may be off-limits because the drain will freeze.

Anyone who rides on your property, even under the most casual of circumstances, must sign a liability waiver and wear a helmet.

tip 24.

Owning a horse often involves entering into business relationships. Avoid legal problems by getting everything in writing. In this litigious society, common sense dictates that anyone who rides your horses or rides on your property should sign a liability waiver as a matter of course. Although you may trust your best friend not to sue you if she falls off your pony and breaks a wrist, her health insurance provider may consider you liable and try to force you to pay her hospital bills.

If you lease a horse to or from someone, the lease agreement should cover the amount of the fee and when it is due each month; who is responsible for the cost of board, farrier, routine and emergency vet care, tack, and showing and transportation fees; and whether the lessee may take the horse off the property and under what circumstances.

Boarding contracts should cover the cost of board and what is included in that price; contingency plans for emergencies; what steps management may take if board is not paid (such as selling the horse to recoup expenses); minimum health requirements for horses (usually current Coggins tests and vaccinations); rules regarding outside trainers, instructors, and riders; and a list of the barn rules (see tip 22).

Inspect fences regularly for damage that could injure horses or allow them to escape.

tip 25. If you have wood fences on your

property, you know that horses can and do routinely damage them by chewing the top rail or breaking the fence by leaning out to reach grass on the other side. To discourage these kinds of problems, a single strand of electric fence tape run along the top rail is a wise investment.

Check all your fencing regularly. If some areas of your pasture are not readily visible due to the obstruction of trees, hills, or distance, take a page from the cowboy's book and go out "riding fence" once a week. Check for loose boards, rotting posts, downed electric tape, or electric fence that may have been shorted out by tall grass or weeds. Consider it a good excuse for a trail ride.

tip 26. Plan a weekly stable maintenance

schedule. In addition to your daily chores, designate each day of the week for special once-a-week tasks. A sample schedule might look something like this:

Monday: Scrub out all grain buckets.

Tuesday: Sweep cobwebs out of rafters and corners.

Wednesday: Sweep, rotate, and restock hay and feed room.

Thursday: Clean tack.

Friday: Check and repair fencing.

Saturday: Check and turn manure compost piles.

Sunday: Pick out paddocks and run-in sheds.

tip 27.

"A good barn manager maintains opening and closing hours," counsels Mott Atherholt. "Horses and people both need rest and quiet."

A set time, such as 9 a.m., for opening will give you a chance to feed, water, turn horses out, clean stalls, and attend to other business without boarders interrupting or getting in the way. Asking boarders to vacate the facilities at a certain hour in the evening will ensure that horses get their needed relaxation time, prevent unpleasant late-night noise from the barn, and save your electric bill because all stable and arena lights will be turned off.

Muck buckets hanging on each horse's stall door make it convenient to pick out stalls as needed. (Courtesy of Caroline Dowd)

tip 28.

When horses have been inside for all or part of the day due to bad weather or other factors, their stalls become quite messy by bedtime. In addition to your regular, thorough daily stall cleaning, pick out stalls in the evening while horses are eating dinner. The chore only takes a few moments, and it has so many benefits. It extends the life of the bedding; it prevents horses from standing, lying, and eating in their manure all night; it saves stall-cleaning time the next day; and it gives you an opportunity to take one last look to make sure everyone's healthy, comfortable, and happy for the night.

Sweep out wet spots and sprinkle them with lime to minimize odors. (Jason Shiers)

tip 29.

Even if you clean your stalls religiously, urine will soak into the flooring material and produce unpleasant and even hazardous ammonia fumes. If walking into a pungent stall on a rainy day makes you wince, imagine how your horse must feel living in there. Over time, ammonia fumes can damage his throat and lungs.

In stalls with dirt floors, sprinkle hydrolyzed lime over the "wet spot" each day after removing all soaked bedding to neutralize the ammonia. If horses are not in their stalls, let the wet spot air-dry for a few hours before replacing the bedding. Strip rubber-matted stalls once a week, sweep out all soiled bedding, and replace it with fresh, clean shavings.

Bonus tip: Every month (more often during the summer), lift the edges of the mats to check for soiled bedding that has worked its way underneath. This is often the source of the worst odors. Scrape the offending bedding out and sprinkle some lime under the mats.

Horses need high-quality, safe drinking water. Test your well regularly to make sure it's not contaminated.

tip 30.

Wells, the water source on most farms, should be tested periodically for bacteria, impurities, pH level, radium, minerals, and salt content. Test wells annually for coliform bacteria and parasites in the water that can come from septic or manure contamination, and sterilize them with bleach if necessary. Determine the source of the contamination, such as a septic tank or manure pile located too close to the well, and take any necessary steps to prevent it. Install a filter to help eliminate other impurities, and treat the water to regulate pH balance.

Wells near roadways may become contaminated by runoff of chemicals and salt from the road in the winter. The resulting high mineral and salt content can be difficult to manage. Consult with your county's agricultural extension office for further information if your well has this problem.

When the **horse's** jaws are in motion, his mind is at **rest.**

—Pete Rose

George is happily enjoying his dinner—despite the rocks.

tip 31.

If your horse tends to wolf his grain, which can lead to gas colic or choke, you can slow him down by placing three or four fist-sized, smooth stones in his grain bucket. Wash them thoroughly first. He'll then be forced to search for the grain by moving the rocks around, which will make him take a longer time to eat.

Bonus tip: Another tactic is to feed hay about twenty minutes before you feed grain to take the edge off his hunger. Then he won't be so frantic about the grain, which will pass more slowly through the gut so the horse can absorb the most nutrients possible.

---

tip 32.

Knowing your horse's weight is useful when calculating dosage for wormers, supplements, and medications. Overdosing will waste some of the expensive product, and may even threaten your horse's health. If you underdose, the horse will not get the maximum benefit of the medication. Check your horse's weight once a month. When you see him every day, it's hard for your eyes to register any gradual changes in his overall condition.

A weight tape, readily available at most tack shops, is an easy way to find out how much your horse weighs and to get an early warning of weight loss or gain. It's not exact, but will provide a reasonable estimate. For best results, stand the horse square on level ground. Wrap the weight tape snugly around the horse's heartgirth just behind the elbow when he exhales. Take several measurements and then use the average as your final weight.

Bonus tip: This formula provides a more precise estimate:

Heartgirth (inches) x Heartgirth (inches) x Length (inches, from center of chest to point of croup) ÷ 300 = Weight (pounds)

---

tip 33. Take your hay's temperature.

Damp hay can start to ferment, causing the internal temperature of a bale or stack to rise. Several problems result: The hay becomes moldy and unpalatable, unfit to be fed to horses. The heat causes the carbohydrates in the hay to break down, reducing its nutritional value. In the worst-case scenario, the internal temperature of a large stack of baled hay can become so high that the hay spontaneously ignites and causes a barn fire.

To prevent these problems, check the temperature of individual bales by slipping your hand between the flakes; the hay should feel cool. Regularly check the temperature of stored, stacked hay by inserting a metal pipe several feet into the middle of the stack. Dangle a thermometer on the end of a string into the pipe and let it hang there for fifteen minutes, as it adjusts to the ambient temperature of the haystack. A temperature in excess of 150 degrees Fahrenheit is in danger of spontaneous combustion. Immediately unload the hay from the barn and divide the hay into smaller piles in a well-ventilated area.

Draft breeds often don't need any grain at all, especially when they live on lush pasture. This handsome gentleman could stand to lose a little weight. (photos.com)

tip 34. A simple horseman's rule of thumb

regarding equine weight is that you should be able to feel but not see the horse's ribs. If you have to press hard to feel the ribs, then the horse is overweight. Many owners feed grain to all of their horses, but not all horses need grain. Many ponies and draft horses or draft crosses do best on hay, grass, and only a handful of grain or no grain at all. A horse that is in very light work may also not need grain.

The dangers of horses being overweight are many—including increased risk of heat stress and increased strain on joints and tendons—but laminitis is chief among them. Laminitis, also known as founder, is a life-threatening disease in which the *laminae* (supporting structures in the hoof wall) break down, allowing rotation of the coffin bone, which results in severe hoof pain. Fat horses are at a much greater risk of foundering due to the greater load on the laminae. However, if your horse is so overweight that you have trouble feeling his ribs, do not simply eliminate grain all at once. Discuss the matter with your vet and wean the horse off grain slowly, because putting the horse on a "starvation diet" can cause liver problems.

bran nuggets.

Guaranteed Lysine level ensures quality protein is available for strong muscle development and maintenance of body tissues.

A Unique Advanced Antioxidant Package containing Natural Tocopherols and added Vitamin E helps to maintain the integrity of cells and tissues by neutralizing damaging free-radicals produced during intense exercise. The benefits of antioxidation on vital systems leads to a lifetime of good health and activity.

Guaranteed Analysis

Crude Protein, Min.	10.0%
Lysine, Min.	0.5%
Crude Fat, Min.	10.0%
Crude Fiber, Max.	11.0%
Calcium, Min.	0.60% Max. 1.10%
Phosphorus, Min.	0.6%
Copper, Min.	42 ppm
Selenium, Min.	0.5 ppm
Zinc, Min.	140 ppm
Vitamin A, Min.	5000 IU/lb
Vitamin E, Min.	85 IU/lb

Ingredients

Steamed Crimped Oats, Corn Germ, Beet Pulp, Wheat Middlings, Cane Molasses, Vegetable Oil, Stabilized Rice Bran, Soybean Hulls, Yeast Culture, Wheat Flour, Monocalcium Phosphate, Calcium Carbonate, L-Lysine Monohydrochloride, Salt, Magnesium Oxide, Potassium Chloride, Manganese Sulfate, Manganese Proteinate, Cobalt Carbonate, Calcium Iodate, Calcium Propionate, Zinc Sulfate, Zinc Proteinate, Copper Sulfate, Copper Proteinate, Ferrous Sulfate, Sodium Selenite

Don't ignore the labels on your grain bags. These details are important to your horse's health. (Jason Shiers)

tip 35. Pay attention to percentages of

fat, carbohydrates, and protein in your horse's grain. The main sources of energy are carbohydrates and fats. In grain, carbohydrates are made up of sugars and starches. In hay and grass, they come from cellulose fiber. Carbohydrates from sugars are an easily digestible energy source and can make "hot" horses even more high-strung. Fats are the oils in the grain, hay, and grass. For optimum performance and digestive health, grain should be no higher than 12 percent fat. Diets with more than 15 percent fat can cause loose stools and do not improve performance over grain with 12 percent fat.

The ideal percentage of protein for maintenance and exercise for most horses is 8 to 12 percent. Too little protein leads to weight loss, reduced endurance, poor hair coat and hoof quality, and lack of appetite. Because protein cannot be stored in the body, any excess protein is excreted in urine. Horses eating too much protein will have darker and stronger-smelling urine and will drink more water.

"Is it a scoop? Is it a quart? I don't know!"

tip 36. Feed by weight, not volume. Most

owners and barn managers feed grain by volume, using a measuring scoop. This practice can lead to inconsistencies in rations for many reasons. One bag of grain may be a bit more settled than another, thus containing less air and more grain per scoop. The person who feeds on Mondays may consider a "scoop" to be a heaping, rounded scoop, while the Tuesday feeder thinks a scoop should be level (and don't even get me started on the problems with calculating half a scoop).

I once worked in a vet barn where all horses were fed by weight. In the feed room was a hanging scale, exactly like those in the supermarket produce aisle. Using such a scale is easy and almost error-proof. You'll waste much less grain by not accidentally overfeeding, and you'll know that your horses are being fed the right amount, every time, no matter who feeds.

If baled hay has been allowed to stand in the field for too long, the nutrients may be leached out by the sun and rain, leaving the hay with a brown or yellow color. (photos.com)

tip 37.

Although we all know that hay quality is important, many owners don't know exactly what to look for in a bale of hay. A visual appraisal will tell you a lot about its quality. Look for the following four characteristics:

- Maturity: Hay that's harvested at the right time will have a high proportion of grassy leaves and few or no strawlike stems and seedheads (seeds and stems indicate that the hay was harvested after it had entered its reproductive phase and has lost a good deal of its nutrients).

- Condition: Never buy hay that looks or smells dusty or moldy or is damp. Very heavy bales, which usually contain too much moisture, will become moldy in time and can cause barn fires (see tip 33).

- Color: Good hay is green hay. A green color indicates the presence of vitamins such as carotene. Hay that is brown or bleached is generally lower quality and has fewer nutrients.

- Purity: Each bale should be free of foreign material such as sticks, weeds, and garbage.

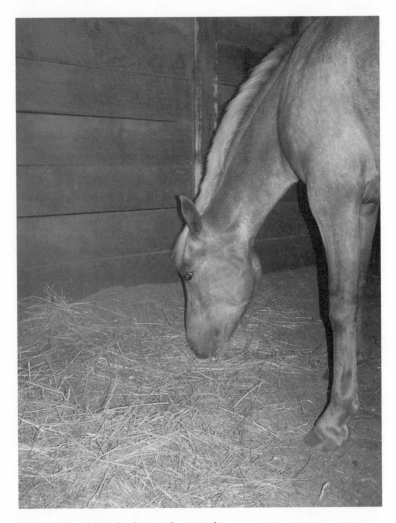

Cinnamon is enjoying her hay on the ground.

tip 38.

Feed hay on the ground. This is the horse's natural position when grazing, and it also prevents him from inhaling dust and chaff that can drift down from hay feeders. If you are feeding outdoors on sandy soil (see tip 42) or in a stall where hay may become mixed with dirty bedding, install a rubber mat to feed on. Sweep the mat clean before each feeding. If your horse routinely uses one part of his stall or pen as a "toilet" area, take that fact into consideration when choosing the site for his dinner area.

These bins—which are rodent-, moisture-, and horse-proof when closed and locked—are ideal for grain storage.

tip 39.

As grazing animals that, in nature, browse constantly throughout the day, horses do not have the ability to gauge when they are "full." Given the opportunity, they may literally eat themselves to death. For this reason, a horse should not be able to get at the grain if he escapes from his stall. Keep grain locked away in a designated and secure feed room. Store grain in sealed, rodent-proof bins where mice and other wildlife can't litter it with their droppings. (Opossums, carriers of a parasite called Equine Protozoal Myeloencephalitis, or EPM, are the most dangerous grain invaders; see tip 62.) Keep the feed room and bins dry and clean to avoid mold or rancidity. As new bags of grain are delivered, rotate the older bags so they are used first.

Bonus tip: It's best to store tack and feed in separate rooms to discourage mice from setting up housekeeping among your saddle pads.

It's a dirty job, but somebody's got to do it. (Jason Shiers)

tip 40.

Water and grain buckets in stalls and in paddocks quickly become unhealthily foul if not maintained daily. Bits of grain and hay can fester at the bottom of a water bucket, and the sides of the bucket are a host for algae and bacteria. Bird droppings may accumulate in barns, and mosquitoes love to breed in the standing water of a paddock stock tank. Empty, scrub out, and refill water buckets every day.

At least once a week in winter and daily in summer, scrub grain buckets with hot water, then dry them with a clean towel to keep away bacteria, rancid feed, and flies. If you feed a wet grain such as beet pulp or mash, rinse buckets after every feeding.

Oleander is a beautiful flowering shrub that is often used in gardening and landscaping. One ounce of its leaves can kill a horse. (photos.com)

tip 41. Know the poisonous plants in your

region and check for them, both in your pastures and in your hay. Among the many common plants that are toxic to horses are poison hemlock, tansy ragwort, field horsetail, buttercups, yellow star thistle, lupines, yew, oleander, bracken fern, Saint-John's-wort, and nightshade. Check with a nearby university's agricultural extension to find out about specific poisonous plants in your area. It's not always possible to eliminate all such plants from horse pastures, so the best way to prevent poisoning is to make sure horses have plenty of grass and hay to keep them satisfied. Horses will usually avoid eating poisonous plants that are in their pastures, but they may consume them if the grass gets too low or they get bored or curious. It's a risk you don't want to take.

If you suspect your horse may have eaten a poisonous plant, call the vet immediately. Some symptoms may include frothing at the mouth, lethargy, or neurological symptoms such as stumbling, incoordination, and muscle spasms. Unfortunately, the first "symptom" of poisoning is often the sudden unexpected death of a horse. In other cases, symptoms only appear once long-term neurological damage has become so severe that the horse cannot be saved. Again, the best plan is to make sure horses never have a reason or opportunity to eat the plants at all.

tip 42.
Horses who live and graze in sandy pastures or who are fed their hay directly on sandy soil can accidentally ingest quite a bit of sand. Sand does not easily pass through the horse's digestive system. It can collect in the twists and turns of the intestines and lead to an impaction known as *sand colic.*

To find out whether your horse is ingesting sand, conduct the Rubber Glove Test. Get a transparent rubber glove, the bigger the better (the best kind to use, for ease of handling, are the arm-length veterinary kind). Collect two or three manure balls and put them in the glove. Fill it with water, tie off the wrist end, and let it hang, fingers-down, for twenty-four hours. Then check the fingertips for sand by sight or by feeling. If you can see or feel a mass of sand grains, then the horse has obviously been ingesting sand, which is probably collecting in his intestines just like it did in the fingertips of the glove.

If it's not possible to move the horse off the sandy ground for feeding, then start giving him a psyllium supplement or other anti-sand supplement once a week.

The plow rests in the winter, the sleigh in the summer, the **horse never.**

—Yiddish proverb

Alfie Moon, a Gypsy Cob imported from Ireland, grows a long coat in the winter and never needs a blanket.

tip 43. To blanket or not to blanket? That

is the question. Everyone seems to have a different opinion on the topic of blanketing in the winter. For starters, whether to blanket depends on your geographic location. If you happen to live in Miami, then no, you do not need to blanket your horses. Ever.

Breed is also a factor. A shaggy Shetland pony who sports a coat like a grizzly bear's from November through April doesn't need a blanket—even if he lives in New England. In fact, a blanket would do more harm than good, as it would flatten down his naturally fluffy coat, reducing its insulating and water-resisting properties.

For the average-coated or clipped horse in the temperate zones, a good rule of thumb is that if you need to wear a sweater, throw a sheet on your horse. If you need a sweater and a jacket, use a medium-weight blanket. If you need a parka, scarf, mittens, hat, and wool socks, he needs a heavy turnout rug.

Lay the blanket high up on the withers before sliding it back into place. (Jason Shiers)

tip 44.

When blanketing, fasten and buckle from front to back. If you clip on the hind leg straps first and the horse moves before you've had a chance to fasten the chest buckles, the blanket could slip off and become tangled under his hind feet.

The sequence for safe and comfortable blanketing is first to fold the blanket in half crosswise, bringing the tail flap up to meet the withers area, inside out. Lay the folded blanket high up on the withers so that it's too far forward, then unfold it carefully, laying the back end smoothly over his haunches.

Buckle the chest straps first, taking care that they are loose enough to allow the horse to comfortably lower his head when he eats. Now move to the back of the horse and pull the blanket smoothly backward into place so the horse's hair lies flat under it (this prevents chafing and keeps the hair shiny and smooth).

Next, cross the surcingles under the horse's belly. The straps should be loose enough to fit a hand underneath, but not so loose that he could catch a hind foot under one if he scratches or rolls.

Finally, clip on the hind leg straps. Whether you cross them between the hind legs or loop each one around a leg and clip it to the same side is a matter of personal preference and the fit of the individual blanket. I find that crossing them keeps the blanket more secure, but some people feel that clipping to the same side minimizes chafing. Whichever method keeps your horse's blanket secure and comfortable is fine—as long as the straps are loose enough not to rub and short enough to avoid tangling a leg.

tip 45.

People who live in a cold climate may wake up to more than one morning of frozen-solid water buckets. An easy way to deal with this problem is to use black rubber buckets (as opposed to plastic, which may crack when the water freezes). Set the frozen buckets out in the sun alongside the barn wall, where they can absorb the most possible sunlight, before you begin your barn chores.

However, buckets must be black for this to work. Black absorbs the sun's rays better than any other color. By the time you've finished feeding, turning out, mucking, and sweeping, the buckets should be defrosted at least to the point that you can dump out the chunks of ice, scrub the buckets, and refill them with fresh warm water.

This automatic waterer provides fresh, ice-free water in all but the coldest weather. (Jason Shiers)

tip 46.

Dehydration is a good way to bring on a bout of impaction colic during the winter, because horses don't like to drink frigid water. (Can you blame them?) To make sure your horses always have ready access to palatable water, invest in a water tank heater for the pasture and heated or insulated buckets for your stalls. Now readily available through most feed stores or catalogs, these gadgets more than make up for their cost in the time and energy you save by not having to heat and haul warm water out to the barn all winter. In addition, horses are much more willing to drink the room-temperature water provided by the heaters than to sip ice water through the crust of frost that inevitably develops overnight.

tip 47. A thousand-pound horse should

drink eight to ten gallons of water a day. If you find that your horses aren't drinking enough, try adding a few ounces of a flavored sports drink, such as Gatorade, to each bucket. Not only does it improve the flavor, but it also adds electrolytes that a horse's body needs to absorb and process water efficiently. Also provide a bucket of pure water as an option in case your finicky horse decides the Gatorade-flavored version tastes bad.

Alternatively, Mott Atherholt suggests that you "float an apple in the water bucket. It will help make the water seem tastier to the horse, and may encourage him to drink more water while 'bobbing' for the apple."

Bonus tip: During the hot summer months, horses lose a lot of sodium and water through sweating. Adding a couple of teaspoons of table salt to a horse's grain will replace the lost sodium and will whet his thirst, encouraging him to drink more.

---

tip 48.

On those long, humid days when horses sweat just standing in their stalls, they will appreciate a nice, cold hose-down. Although it may seem that leaving them really wet will help them stay cool, the opposite is true. Water trapped under the hair acts as an insulator and actually holds in heat. Instead, scrape the horse down thoroughly after a bath to remove the hot water. (Feel the temperature of the water as you scrape it off—it's really hot!) Repeat the rinsing and scraping several times to draw off as much body heat as possible, until the water that runs off is cool.

A round pen can work double duty as a sacrifice turnout area for one or two horses while your pastures rest.

tip 49. One of the most efficient ways to

kill grass, tear up the topsoil, and turn your pastures into mud pits is to turn horses out when the grass is young or the ground is saturated. Horse hooves are notoriously destructive to soft ground. To keep your pastures healthy and pleasant, use a *sacrifice area*—a designated paddock area near the barn where you do not expect grass to grow. Keep horses in these smaller paddocks any time you feel your pasture's health is at risk. Such times might include mud season, after a hard rain, when the grass has been eaten down too much, or in the fall when the grass has stopped growing.

As a rule of thumb, turn horses out in the spring only once the grass has grown to over 6 inches in height. By this time, the root systems will have developed enough to protect the ground from hooves, and the grass is mature and plentiful enough to survive grazing. Waiting also prevents the horses from eating too much of the young, early-spring grasses that contain high levels of *fructan*, the sugar that has been linked to laminitis (for more on laminitis, see tip 63).

This overhead oscillating fan, with the cord tied safely above, provides relief from the heat while staying well out of L.B.'s reach.

tip 50. When it's extremely hot—over 85

degrees Fahrenheit—keep horses inside during the day, where they are sheltered from the sun and flies, and turn them out only at night. If you're not comfortable leaving them outside all night, then bite the bullet and get up at 4:00 a.m. to turn them out, then bring them in by 10:00 or 11:00 a.m., before the heat becomes oppressive.

Fans in stall windows help bring relief, as long as you are careful to rig them so there's no risk of an electrical fire. Keep the cords out of reach of curious horse lips, and clean the fans frequently to keep dust out of the motor (another potential fire hazard). The breeze will also help keep flies at bay.

Snow can be dangerous if it builds up and forms ice balls in a horse's hooves. (Jason Shiers)

tip 51.

Anyone who lives in the northern climes knows the hazards of snow balling up in a horse's hooves during turnout or while riding outdoors. To help combat this icy buildup, spread a thin layer of Vaseline onto the sole of each hoof before riding or turning horses out on snow. The Vaseline will prevent the snow from sticking to the sole. Avoid the edges of the hoof wall (if the horse is barefoot) or the shoe (if he is shod): you don't want to compromise his traction.

Alfie doesn't wear shoes in the winter. And look how happy he is!

tip 52.

If horses will not be in much work during the winter or if they will only be ridden in the snow, consider pulling their shoes for the snowy season. Because they will only be working on soft, snowy surfaces, if at all, they don't need the protection of shoes.

Many farriers and horsemen believe that giving horses a yearly break from shoes benefits the long-term health of hooves, allowing them to grow into their natural shape. In addition, bare hooves will find better traction on slippery surfaces than shod hooves will.

Always discuss this decision with your vet and farrier first, however; some horses, such as those being treated for navicular disease, have special needs and should wear shoes all the time.

My experience of horses is that they never throw away a chance to **go lame.**

–Mark Twain

tip 53.

One of the most important things you can do for the health and safety of your horses is to educate yourself about all aspects of equine care. Read books about horse-keeping. Subscribe to magazines that can keep you informed on the latest developments in veterinary research. Take advantage of university agricultural extensions for region-specific information on plants, wildlife, hay-growing, and feeding concerns. Learn about all kinds of injuries, diseases, skin conditions, and nutrient deficiencies so you can take steps to prevent them if possible—and so you will recognize the symptoms if they occur in your own horses. Know what to do in case of emergencies. The more you know, the safer and healthier your horses will be.

tip 54.

Keep a large wall calendar in the tack room to make note of wormings, vaccinations, farrier's visits, massage therapist visits, upcoming shows or events, feed deliveries, and so on. You can also use this calendar to note health problems as they develop. For example, every morning take the temperature of a horse being treated for a virus and record it on the calendar. When you weight-tape your horses each month, note their weights on the calendar as well (see tip 32).

To simplify life, keep all horses on the same schedule for worming, vaccinations, and farrier. New horses moving into the stable may be on different routines, but slowly you can wean them onto your standardized schedule. For example, all horses will be dewormed on the first of every other month; the farrier comes on the fifteenth of every month; all horses are vaccinated on the same day in the spring and in the fall.

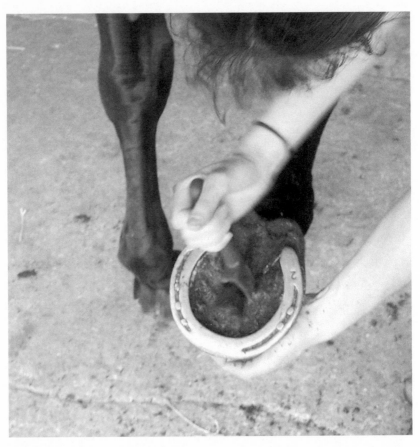

I like to use a hoof pick with a brush built in, so I can brush out the grooves on either side of the frog. (Jason Shiers)

tip 55.

Clean your horse's hooves every day. That's *every day*—even if you don't ride. Keeping hooves clean keeps them healthy. As you pick them out each day, you'll notice any developing problems—such as thrush, a stone, or a loose shoe—before they become major problems.

You'll recognize the beginning stages of thrush by its foul odor and the soft, black and white crumbly material in the sole and frog. Keep a bottle of anti-thrush remedy handy to quickly treat thrush and prevent it from getting worse. Evidence of thrush is a cue to review your stable management practices. Clean stalls more thoroughly and add more fresh, dry bedding, or move horses out of muddy pastures and paddocks.

A fly sheet and fly mask protect Jaguar from biting insects that can cause hives.

tip 56.

Horses develop hives for a variety of reasons, typically as an allergic reaction. Hives, which are bumps on the skin that look like welts, vary in size from bug-bite size to half-dollar size. They may or may not be itchy or oozing, and may be localized or may cover the horse's whole body.

When you spot hives, first try to determine the cause. Consider any new materials that the horse may have been in contact with: bedding, feed, horse clothing, laundry detergent, sprays, or bath products. Some horses, for example, are allergic to the citronella found in natural fly sprays. If you can determine the source of the problem, immediately remove it. If the hives are caused by insect bites, turn the horse out only at night or use a fly sheet.

In the meantime, apply witch hazel or calamine lotion topically to help ease itching and dry out any ooze. In an extreme case, the vet may administer an antihistamine injection.

tip 57.

A good indication of a horse's health is the quality of his manure. Dry manure may indicate dehydration or an impaction. Wet, mushy manure can simply mean that the horse is nervous or unsettled, which often occurs when a horse travels or moves to a new stable. However, if this occurs on a regular basis, it can be a sign that the horse's diet is too high in fat. If manure is otherwise normal but the horse seems to have the "runs" (the manure is followed by a watery discharge), he may have a problem in the hind gut, which a probiotic supplement can help. If manure contains whole, undigested grains, check the horse's teeth, or consider switching to a more easily digested feed such as a senior feed.

Bonus tip: Also take note of any wads of unchewed hay that you may find in the stall. Elderly horses or horses with bad teeth can't chew hay well enough to swallow it, so they end up spitting it back out in wads, a behavior known as *quidding*. If you find these wads, call the dentist for a floating and consider switching to alfalfa cubes or a bagged, chopped hay product.

tip 58.
Keep a file on each horse with thorough records of all vaccinations, tooth floatings, hoof care, and veterinary care. This way, you will know when those services are due again. If your horse suffers a puncture wound, the vet will ask you whether the horse's tetanus vaccinations are up to date. If you don't know, he'll have to administer another one, costing you money. Or if there is an outbreak of the highly contagious disease *strangles* in your stable, you will know immediately which horses have been vaccinated for it and which should be quarantined. When you decide to sell a horse, the buyer will want proof that the horse has been well cared for and is up to date on its vaccinations, tooth care, and farrier care.

tip 59.

Listen to your horse. A horse that is ill or in pain can't just tell you in so many words. You must be alert to his body language and aware of his normal patterns of behavior so you'll notice when something is amiss. For example, if your horse is usually bouncing at the end of the lead line as you bring him out to his pasture, but today he is mellow and sleepy, don't congratulate yourself on finally having taught him to walk quietly. Bring him back to the barn and take his temperature—something is probably wrong.

Here is a case history: a normally pleasant and well-behaved horse became progressively more irritable, dancing around, kicking, and biting when his owner tried to curry him. Under saddle, he developed an unpleasant and dangerous habit of bolting when asked to canter. The owner wrote this off as bad behavior and thought the horse was just being naughty.

During the horse's biannual floating, the dentist discovered that at the previous floating, a vet with a power floater had accidentally gouged a molar. In the intervening six months, the damaged tooth developed a nasty and painful abscess. This was the root of what was perceived as naughtiness: the dancing and kicking were his way of complaining that he was in pain, and his bolting under saddle was an attempt to run away from the agony caused by bit pressure.

A little corrective dental work and a course of antibiotics soon had horse and owner back on the road to happiness.

tip 60.

If you know the feeling of your horse's normal digital pulse, you'll be aware when something is wrong. Learn how to find it and check it regularly.

To locate the digital pulse, place your index finger around the outer side of the fetlock joint at its lower edge. Applying gentle pressure with your finger, run your finger from side to side around the fetlock joint until you feel a bundle of veins, nerves, and arteries underneath your touch. Apply pressure to this bundle for five to ten seconds until you feel a pulse. If you can't find a pulse, you may be pressing too hard and cutting off the blood flow. Or you may be pressing too lightly to feel the pulse at all. Adjust the pressure until you feel the pulse.

A normal digital pulse is quite faint and may be difficult if not impossible to feel. If you can easily feel the pulse and it seems to be throbbing, there may be a problem. A strong digital pulse can indicate an abscess that needs treatment or, worse, the beginnings of founder.

tip 61. Is it an emergency? Always call

the vet in the following cases:

- Joint capsule is involved in injury (you'll see a honey-colored, stringy discharge; this is the synovial fluid.)

- Eye injury

- Horse is not putting weight on a leg or is lame at the walk

- You can't identify the source of a lameness

- You suspect a broken bone

- Bleeding won't stop

- Colic symptoms (kicking, biting, or looking at stomach; rolling; pawing; sweating; not eating)

- Laminitis symptoms (lame in front, heat in soles, strong digital pulse)

- Elevated temperature (over 101 degrees), respiratory rate, or pulse

- When in doubt

This is the ugly little guy who carries the EPM parasite. (photos.com)

tip 62. Equine Protozoal Myeloencephali-

tis (EPM) is a parasite spread by opossums. It attacks the central nervous system of a horse, causing *ataxia* (incoordination of the legs), in
some cases necessitating euthanasia if the horse becomes too unco-
ordinated to walk or stand. To reduce the risk of your horses contract-
ing EPM, take these steps to keep opossums away from your stable:

- Keep feed storage areas as clean as possible: Put grain in tightly
  closed containers and keep hay storage areas clean. Cover hay
  with a tarp and remove or tightly cover any food (including cat
  and dog food) or garbage.

- Use wire mesh fencing with an electric fence wire strung around
  the outside to discourage opossums from climbing over it.

- If you already have opossums on your property, trap and relo-
  cate them with a humane trap, using peanut butter, fruit, or
  cookies as a lure. Be sure to check with wildlife or animal con-
  trol officers for your area's regulations governing trapping and
  relocating opossums.

tip 63.

Unless you must do so to avoid extreme heat in the summer, don't turn horses out at dawn or dusk. As a rule of thumb, wait until the sun has dried the dew before turning out in the morning, and bring horses inside before the sun sets in the evening.

There are two health-related reasons. One is to avoid exposing your horses to mosquitoes, which are most active at dusk. Mosquitoes transmit West Nile virus, a fatal infection of the nervous system that can affect birds, horses, and humans. Since its initial appearance in 1999, West Nile has spread throughout the continental United States. Although there is now a vaccine available for horses in high-risk geographical areas, limiting exposure to mosquitoes is a wise idea.

A second reason is that an element of rich grass known as *fructan* has been implicated as a precipitating cause of laminitis (founder). Tests have shown that fructan levels are highest in grasses during cool seasons just before the dew has dried or just after it has fallen (i.e., dawn or dusk). If a horse is prone to founder, restricting his access to grass at these times can help avoid a recurrence.

tip 64. Invest in health insurance for your

horses. For most owners, major medical and mortality is the most practical option. Benefits accrue only if your horse needs surgery or other major medical procedures—or if (heaven forbid) he dies, you will then be compensated for the loss. Routine vet expenses and smaller costs are typically not covered, but monthly premiums are lower than for more complete coverage, which can be prohibitively expensive.

If any horse health insurance at all seems like an extravagance, consider this: if your child's beloved pony colics badly, are you prepared to make the decision between spending several thousand dollars out of your own pocket for surgery versus allowing the pony to die?

I didn't think so.

Caroline and her mare Lazy Dot competed at the Badminton CCI**** event in England in 1999. To get to this level, one has to know a lot about horsekeeping! (Courtesy of Caroline Dowd)

tip 65. Caroline Dowd often has new

horses moving into her Quarter Run Farm in North Carolina. New horses always bring with them the risk of communicable diseases such as strangles. To avoid the possible spread of disease, Caroline observes the following system:

"Before the new horse arrives, strip out his stall, disinfect the stall walls and floor with Lysol or a similar product, and use new bedding. Disinfect grain and water buckets and leave them outside in the sun to dry. Using a broad spectrum wormer, worm the new horse before he steps off the trailer. Then quarantine the new horse for ten days. This gives time to observe the horse for possible communicable diseases. Do not allow the new horse to get close enough to touch any other horse, especially to touch noses."

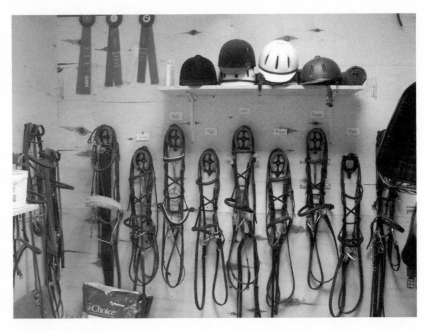

A well-organized tack room, with each horse's bridle clearly labeled.

tip 66.

To prevent the spread of skin diseases, each horse in a stable should have his or her own grooming supplies, blankets, saddle pads, and leg wraps. "Each horse should have its own set of grooming tools kept together in a suitable container. Sharing grooming tools is a health hazard," Mott Atherholt says. "Be sure to mark each grooming box with the horse's name." This becomes especially important in a lesson stable, where the horses are often ridden by riders who don't know which brush belongs to which pony. To further keep items separate, as well as to provide order and prevent misplaced equipment, Mott recommends "a designated place for each horse's tack and equipment. That space should be marked clearly with the horse's name."

tip 67.

The least expensive and most useful first aid equipment you can buy is a hose. Any time your horse has a leg injury that involves slight heat and swelling, spend twenty minutes running a light stream of cold water over it twice a day.

Cold hosing is beneficial for bruises, splints, kicks, stocking up, tendon and ligament injuries . . . whenever swelling and heat are present. Cold water draws the heat out of the leg and takes the swelling down, just as icing an injury does for humans. This treatment, which helps alleviate the horse's discomfort, will also help reduce potential long-term tissue and joint damage caused by the inflammation.

If the swelling and heat are severe or the horse is lame, do call your vet first. But when in doubt, cold hosing never hurts. Dry the legs thoroughly afterward using a towel and even a hair dryer on the low setting in cold weather (if the horse will tolerate it). If the water stays on his legs, he could develop a fungal skin infection.

tip 68.

Learn how to wrap a standing bandage and make sure you have the right supplies on hand before you need them. When my first horse came in from the pasture one Sunday evening with a splint, I realized that I had neither quilted wraps nor standing bandages, and even if I did, I wouldn't know how to use them. Fortunately, I managed to find a tack shop that agreed to stay open for me while I drove the half-hour to buy the wraps, and then a friend was kind enough to show me what to do when I got home.

Thinking back on this now, I realize what a ridiculous and unnecessary situation it was. As with any first aid product, buy your wraps *before* you need them, and practice using them. The finished product should look smooth and straight from top to bottom—no bunching or unevenness that can lead to a bandage bow (a swelling of the tendon that runs from the back of the knee to the fetlock). Don't skimp on quality when choosing your quilted wraps. Thick, dense wraps protect your horse's delicate tendons much better than thin, cheap ones.

This is where scratches come from. (Jason Shiers)

tip 69.

You bring your horse in from turnout and begin the task of brushing the caked mud from his fetlock feathers. As you brush, you notice that your horse seems sensitive and irritated. Running your hand over his pasterns and fetlocks, you discover many bumps and scabs. When you pick one off, it brings the hair with it. What is this stuff? The culprit is *scratches*, a fungus that grows in the manure-rich mud of paddocks and pastures and infects the lower legs of horses who stand in the mud. Left untreated, scratches continues to worsen until eventually the whole lower leg swells and the horse becomes lame from the discomfort.

As usual, the best way to deal with scratches is to prevent it. Avoid turning horses out in deep mud. During some parts of the year, however, mud is a fact of life. If your horse has a case of scratches, the remedy is to clean, clip, towel, and treat. First scrub the affected legs with an iodine-based disinfectant and let it stand for several minutes. As you scrub, use your fingers to pick off as many of the scabs as you can. The horse may object—it hurts!—so stay out of kicking range and be gentle. After rinsing thoroughly, use clippers to trim the hair away from the area. Clipping allows the affected skin to dry more quickly, eliminating the moist environment that allows the fungus to grow. Towel the legs until they are as dry as possible. Repeat the io-dine scrubbing, picking, and drying every day until there is no more evidence of scabs or bumps. Keep the horse out of the mud if at all possible, even if this means keeping him in a small paddock or stall, until the scratches are healed.

Bonus tip: If the horse must go out into the mud, you can use Desitin—yes, the diaper rash ointment—to protect the legs.

---

tip 70. A lameness problem that seems

to be localized in the hoof is probably an abscess. There will be no heat, swelling, stiffness, or soreness in the rest of the leg, but the hoof itself will feel warm to the touch, perhaps more in one spot than the rest. After checking the sole of the hoof to confirm that the abscess is not the result of a puncture (if it is, call the vet immediately, and see the Bonus tip on the next page), take the following steps to draw out the infection. Fill a small pail with hot water mixed with Epsom salts. Convince the horse to place his hoof in the pail without dancing around, holding his head and feeding him hay to keep him quiet if you need to. The water must not be above the level of the coronet band (top of the hoof wall), or the heat and salt will actually draw the infection upward—you want it to be drawn down, out of the hoof through the sole. Soak the hoof for twenty minutes.

Meanwhile, ask a friend to hold the horse while you make a thick paste of Betadine and granulated sugar (sugardine). Dry the hoof with a towel, and take care not to set it down unless the floor has been swept clean (you don't want to trap any manure or dirt under the wrap that you're about to make). Using a spatula or your fingers, slop some sugardine onto the sole, concentrating on the area where you feel the most heat. Cover the sugardine with gauze pads or a little sheet cotton. Wrap the entire hoof in Vet-Rap, covering the sole to keep in the sugardine and gauze. Do not turn the horse out while he's wearing this dressing, or it will come off. If the horse seems very sore, you can give him some bute (an anti-inflammatory painkiller available from your vet). However, in this case it's better not to, because as cruel as it may sound, the horse's level of discomfort is the best indication of the status of the abscess. Repeat the soaking and bandaging process the next day. If the horse does not show signs of improvement in three days or if he becomes more sore on the second day, call the vet.

Bonus tip: If the pain turns out to be caused by a puncture and the object is still embedded in the hoof, do not pull it out yourself! The vet needs to take an X-ray to determine the depth and angle of penetration before attempting to remove the object. Pulling it out at the wrong angle could cause greater damage to the hoof.

---

tip 71.

It's early summer, and you've just started turning your new pony out for several hours a day. One evening when she comes in, you notice that the skin on her lips and her nose at the end of her long, white blaze is peeling, flaking, and sensitive to the touch. Could she have eaten a poisonous plant? Is it an allergy of some kind? No—it's just sunburn. Horses and ponies with pink skin under white face markings are prone to sunburn, just as fair-skinned people are. Some horses with freeze brands can also be sunburned where the hair is missing on the brands. Use a high-SPF sunblock on exposed skin before turning horses out. Aloe will soothe any skin that has already burned.

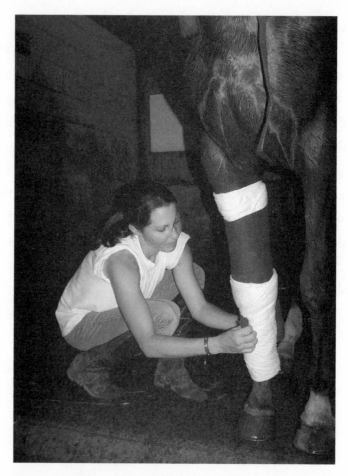

Suzanne is applying a stacked bandage over a poultice to draw the swelling out of Beamer's knee.

tip 72. Since the knee is a joint that

needs to be able to bend, you can't wrap it the same way you would wrap the lower leg. Any normal wrap would loosen and slip down over time. When a horse injures his knee, use a stacked bandage. Wrap the upper leg above the knee first with a quilted wrap and standing bandage, taking care not to wrap too tightly over the accessory carpal bone (the bony point at the back of the knee), which develops pressure sores easily. Then apply a second quilted wrap around the lower part of the leg so it covers the knee and meets the first, upper wrap. Wrap around the quilt with a standing bandage, going only as high as the bottom of the knee joint so you do not impede the joint's action. This technique keeps medication or a poultice in place on the front of the knee, and keeps lacerations covered and clean.

Bonus tip: Stacked bandages are also useful for managing leg inflammation when chest or shoulder injuries cause swelling to drain into the legs from above.

---

tip 73. When your horse is sick and you

call the vet, it helps to have all the key information at hand. Before
you pick up the phone, make note of the answers to the following
questions:

When did you first notice the symptoms?

What is the horse's temperature?

Pulse?

Respiratory rate?

Can you hear normal gut sounds?

Is he eating?

Is he sweating?

Does he show signs of pain—pawing, head tossing, kicking, or
looking at belly?

When did he receive his last course of vaccinations, and which
ones did he have?

tip 74.
Ticks are evil little beasts that latch onto your horse to suck his blood. They cause two main problems. The more important one is that certain species of tick carry Lyme disease. A tick has to stay on an animal for forty-eight hours in order to transmit the disease, which is why checking your horse carefully every day during tick season is so important. Be sure to check all the hidden spots. Ticks especially like to burrow into mane and tail hair, where they are harder to spot during a routine grooming. Pull out the ticks by grabbing them with tweezers as close to the horse's skin as possible, trying not to break off the head. Dab the bite area with peroxide. If you can find the ticks and pull them off immediately, you can help stave off a Lyme outbreak.

The second problem (a less dangerous one, but more immediate) is that horses—unlike dogs, cats, and people—show a very strong response to tick bites. A bite will quickly start to ooze and may be very itchy. The result can be a mane and tail full of nasty, suppurating sores and bald spots from the horse trying to scratch away his itches. The traditional remedy is Listerine mixed with baby oil, a concoction that kills any infection that may be brewing while softening and soothing the crusty sores. It doesn't do much to help the itching, though. To alleviate that problem, you may use topical Benadryl (the kind made for people) on the trouble spots.

There's no fool-proof way to keep ticks from biting. Even the new spot-on treatments will only kill the tick *after* it has bitten—so they help prevent Lyme but won't prevent the scabs. The best things to do are to use plenty of insect repellent on the mane and tail and avoid turning horses out in brushy, wooded areas that harbor ticks.

The kick of a quiet horse strikes strong.

—Armenian proverb

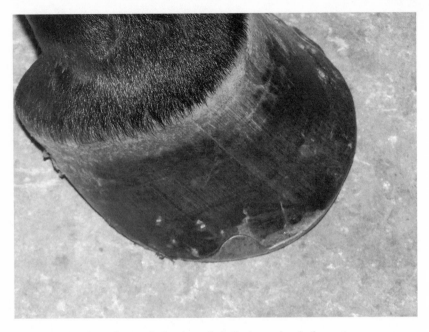

This horse's hoof was damaged when he pulled off a loose shoe in the pasture. (Jason Shiers)

tip 75.

Buy a farrier's clinch cutter and ask your farrier to show you how to use it to remove a horseshoe. It's not difficult and is an essential skill. A loose or twisted shoe must be removed as soon as possible to prevent your horse from injuring himself by tripping or stepping on a loose nail. If a loose shoe tears free on its own, without the nail clinches having been clipped off, the hoof wall suffers unnecessary damage. The basic procedure is to use your clinch cutters to clip off all the nail clinches on the outside of the hoof wall. Then, beginning at the heel and working toward the toe and alternating sides of the shoe, gradually loosen the shoe using the cutters for leverage. At a certain point, provided that all the clinches have been removed, the shoe should drop off. Don't ride or lunge the horse until the farrier resets the shoe.

Bonus tip: If the hoof seems damaged, the horse is uncomfortable, or the farrier won't be able to come out for several days, you can wrap the bare hoof in duct tape or use a temporary horse boot, such as EasyBoots or Old Macs.

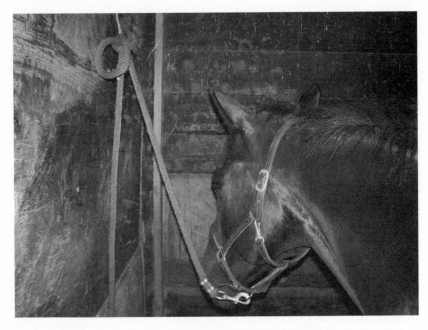

Tie high and short, using a quick-release knot and baling twine. (Jason Shiers)

tip 76.

The structure to which you tie a horse should always be solid and tall. As a rule of thumb, tie a horse at least at the height of his withers, and with a rope that is no longer than your arm (around 2 feet). He should not be able to drop his head to the ground because he may step on or over the rope. Don't tie a horse to a post that the horse can walk around; he may wrap the rope around the post and trap himself.

George is wearing a leather halter for shipping. Baling twine breaks a little too easily to be used when trailering, but notice that the trailer tie is leather and has a panic snap that can be released in an instant in case of an emergency.

tip 77. Whenever you tie your horse,

make sure he can break free in an emergency. Nylon halters and lead lines will not break, and a horse can seriously injure himself if he panics and struggles. I always use a leather halter, or at least a nylon *breakaway* halter with a breakable leather crownpiece. When cross-tying, attach a small loop of baling twine to the cross-tie chain and clip a double-ended snap to the twine. Then snap the other end to the halter. If your horse runs back, he'll break the twine instead of pulling the chain out of the wall, so the chain won't fly back and hit him (or you) in the face. This simple step can avoid a lot of heartache.

Bonus tip: When tying your horse to a tie ring, horse trailer, or post, first tie a piece of twine to the ring, and then tie your lead line to that using a quick-release knot (see tip 78). This kind of knot is the only way a horse should ever be tied, because it is so easy and quick to release in the event of an emergency.

Step 1

Step 2

Step 3

Step 4

tip 78. All horsemen should know how to tie a quick-release knot.

1. Slide the end of the lead rope through your baling twine, leaving about 18 inches on the end that's snapped to the horse's halter. (In the photos, I'm not using baling twine so it's easier for you to see what I'm doing.)

2. Flip the end of the rope over this section, making a keyhole shape.

3. Reach through the keyhole with your left hand and grab the rope, close to the keyhole, and pull it slightly back through, forming a loop.

4. While still holding this loop with your left hand, grab the snap end of the rope and pull it until the keyhole closes tightly around the loop. Give it a good tug to make sure it's secure.

If the horse pulls on this kind of a knot, all he can do is make it tighter and tighter. To release the knot, simply grasp the free end and pull. This will pull the loop back through the keyhole, untying the knot.

He's adorable, but he can wreak havoc in the barn. (photos.com)

tip 79.

Frayed wires can cause a spark when a switch is thrown that, in turn, can start a fire in hay, cobwebs, or bedding. Check barn electrical wiring regularly for fraying caused by natural wear or rodents chewing on the wires. One way to prevent mice from chewing on exposed wires is to wrap the wire in duct tape. Its super-sticky glue will deter rodents from chewing through it. Since it is not a fool-proof method (you can't duct tape every single wire, the glue will eventually dry out, and some mice are just that tenacious), make a visual inspection of your electrical system regularly, ensure that any outlets and connections are clear of cobwebs and other debris, and keep your fuse boxes up to code.

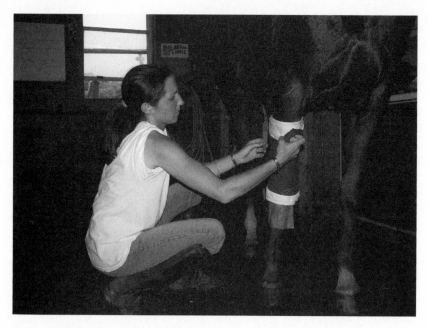

Suzanne keeps her feet on the ground while working near Beamer's legs.

tip 80. Never kneel or sit on the ground

near a horse. If something suddenly startles him, or, worse, if he decides to become aggressive, you will not be able to leap away fast enough to avoid being struck, kicked, or stepped on. Even the most placid of horses should not be taken for granted. If you're kneeling in front of your quiet old retiree while investigating a hoof chip and he stomps at a fly, you could easily be struck in the face by his knee. Instead, squat down while grooming or doctoring the legs, and always keep both feet on the floor. In this position, you are prepared to spring up and back if you need to.

Bonus tip: For additional safety, always keep one hand gently on the nearest leg. You'll feel any sudden motion before you see it, giving you an extra moment to react.

A neat and tidy stall front, with a place for everything and everything in its place. The horse's halter and lead rope are hung on a hook in case of an emergency.

tip 81.

Keep a halter and lead line on every horse's stall door when the horse is in the stall. In case of an emergency such as a barn fire, you won't want to waste time scrambling around trying to find enough lead lines. Keep in mind that it is *not* a good idea to leave halters on horses while they are in their stalls. There are too many opportunities for them to get hung up on something in such close quarters.

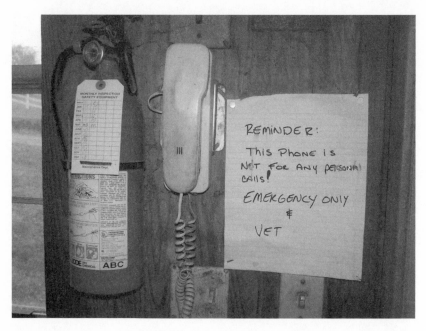

This fire extinguisher is conveniently located next to the barn phone—for emergency use only! (Jason Shiers)

tip 82.

Every barn—no exceptions!—needs a fire extinguisher. Practice using one by aiming it at a cardboard box in the driveway. Or, if local fire regulations allow, set a small, contained fire, ideally in a firepit like the ones in campsites, and practice extinguishing it. This way you won't panic and fumble in an emergency: you'll know what you're doing. (Be sure to have the extinguisher recharged after your test.)

Install battery-operated fire alarms in your barn aisle and hay storage areas and change the batteries twice a year when you change your clocks to or from Daylight Savings Time. Set off the alarms occasionally when the horses are in their stalls so they'll become accustomed to the sound and won't panic in the event of a real fire. Larger facilities should consider investing in a sprinkler system as well.

tip 83.

Each stall should have its own light source, which is beneficial in several ways. If a horse needs emergency care in his stall at night, aisle lights will not provide sufficient illumination to see the horse's condition clearly. Many barns are not lit well enough by natural light to be able to see into the dark corners while cleaning stalls; individual stall lights ensure that no manure or dirty shavings will be overlooked. If you or your boarders are routinely in the stable after dark, you will save electricity by lighting only the stalls that you need, rather than illuminating the entire barn; plus, you won't disturb horses who are resting in the dark. However, any light bulb in a stable, especially those in stalls, *must* be protected by a metal cage. A horse can rear higher than you might imagine, and an exposed light bulb will embed broken glass and possibly a glowing hot wire in the top of a horse's head if he hits it.

tip 84.

In most cases, hand-feeding treats such as carrots and apples helps establish a trusting bond between horse and rider. However, some horses who are hand-fed may become too demanding and aggressive about their treats, which can lead to nipping.

Judy Richter shares how she has handled this behavior in her stable: "We have one greedy, nippy fellow in our barn," she says. "When he gets too pushy about his treats, we offer him a bar of the glycerine soap we use to clean the tack. Having grabbed a few bites in the past, now he only has to smell the soap to know he has stepped over the line. He backs off and stands politely, waiting hopefully for us to forgive him and give him a treat. How much better to deal with him this way than to give him a smack every time he nips and make him head-shy and nervous."

An impeccably clean, tidy, and safe barn aisle at Top Cat Farm.

tip 85. Keep your eyes open. Train your-

self to be always on the lookout for danger. While cleaning a stall, glance around for any splintering wood, loose nails, or broken brackets that can easily cause injury. As you walk through the barn, keep an eye out for dangling halters, scraps of wood, or nails dropped by the shoer. It's much easier to spot and fix or eliminate these objects than it is to care for an infected puncture wound or hoof abscess. One way to spot safety hazards that you may have overlooked is to walk through your stables and pretend you are a visitor. How would a prospective boarder see your barn? Your pasture fences? The cleanliness of your stalls and water buckets?

Bonus tip: Attach a strong magnet to a pole and use it to "sweep" your barn aisles after the farrier's visit. The magnet will pick up any leftover nails.

---

tip 86. Keep two first aid kits in the barn:

one for horses and one for humans. Make sure they are clearly marked and in a convenient location. The horse kit should include:

Veterinarian's phone number

Bandage material: sterile pads, sheet cotton, standing wraps

Disposable diapers for wrapping a hoof

Large-animal thermometer

Phenylbutazone (known as bute, an equine painkiller)

Banamine (a muscle relaxant often used to alleviate colic; ask your vet for banamine and bute)

Antiseptic solution such as Betadine or peroxide

Antiseptic ointment such as Nitrofurazone

Epsom salts

Witch hazel or cortisone ointment for hives

Poultice for swollen legs

Tweezers

Antibiotic eye ointment

Vet-Rap

Twitch

tip 87. The human kit should include:

Band-Aids

Antibiotic ointment

Peroxide

Ibuprofen

Calamine or cortisone lotion

Epi-Pen (an adrenaline injection used by people with life-threatening reactions to bee stings)

Ace bandage

Gauze and bandage tape

Saline solution for rinsing eyes

Ice pack

Scissors or knife

Stethoscope

Flashlight

Leading correctly. Note the folded lead line in my left hand. (Jason Shiers)

tip 88.

The safest way to lead is beside the left shoulder, holding the lead line with your right hand close to the halter. The excess should be folded inside your left hand. *Never* loop a lead line around your hand, even loosely. A horse that suddenly pulls, shies, or rears will tighten the loop, causing at best a rope burn and at worst broken fingers. In fact, I've twice heard of people's thumbs being torn off in this way. If you're leading a nervous or pushy horse that crowds you and tries to step on your feet, extend your right elbow and give him a poke in the neck or shoulder when he comes too close.

Don't drag your horse around or let him drag you. Just as when you are riding, remember that the horse's reward is the release of pressure. If he isn't walking quietly beside you, give a quick tug, either to move him along or slow him down, and then *release* the pressure when he complies. If he doesn't, then tug again, a bit more firmly. If you offer him a steady pull, he will only pull back.

Treat your horses with quiet firmness and they will learn to respect your judgment.
(Betsy Shiers)

tip 89. Keep your cool around your horse.

Try not to get into fights with him. If he challenges you, remain calm and do not allow yourself to become angry or afraid. Remember that although he may be stronger, you will always win if you are smarter and have greater patience. If you really are afraid of your horse and regularly allow him to push you around, consider asking a professional or a more experienced handler for help. A horse that has learned his handler is afraid of him can be unsafe and will likely become more and more aggressive.

Conversely, if you feel yourself losing your temper with a horse, take a step back and take a deep breath. Shouting and hitting will not solve your problems. Your horse will not learn to respect your judgment, but rather will learn to fear and mistrust you, which creates further problems down the road. Take a moment to pause and reflect, and then come back to the challenge at hand with renewed patience and rationality.

Joan Fry's horse Prim and goat Kyle both survived the wildfires unscathed. Note the high, closely woven, goat-friendly fencing. (Joan Fry)

tip 90. Develop a worst-case-scenario emergency plan.

- In case of a barn fire, how will you get all the horses out and where will you contain them? Remember that a horse's instinct when frightened is to return to his comfort zone—his stall. You can't open all the stall doors and expect the horses to flee to safety.

- If you, as the horses' primary caregiver, become very ill or disabled, who will be responsible for the horses in the short- and long-term?

- If you are forced to evacuate from your home, which happened in the Southeast during the record-breaking hurricane season of 2004 and in the Southwest during the raging wildfires of the same year, what will happen to your horses? Will they go with you? If so, where will they stay? If not, how can you make sure they are fed and watered?

Thanks to the kindness of strangers with a horse trailer, Joan Fry, author of *Backyard Horsekeeping*, was able to bring her American Saddlebred, Prim, along for the ride when she had to evacuate from her home in southern California due to wildfires. Unfortunately, she was forced to leave Prim's companion, a little goat named Kyle, at home with water and a pile of hay to fend for himself. When Joan returned home, she was thrilled to discover that Kyle had been cared for and entertained by the firemen who'd been assigned to watch over her property. You can't count on this kind of luck, however. Make sure you have a plan and an informed support team.

tip 91. Stalled horses run the risk of becoming cast, which happens when a horse decides to roll and ends up with his legs so close to the stall wall that he is unable to stand up or roll back over. In this position, horses often either injure themselves by struggling violently or colic due to the prolonged amount of time spent lying down. (Horses normally won't lie down for more than an hour or two at a time. Like beached whales, their digestive processes aren't able to function properly in that position.)

To help prevent this problem, Mott Atherholt recommends that you "bank the stall bedding against the walls to help keep a horse from becoming cast when he rolls." After you clean the stall, fill it with plenty of fresh bedding and use your pitchfork to build banks of 1 to 1.5 feet in height all around each side of the stall. The banks will prevent the horse from getting close enough to the walls to become cast.

Rarely, a horse is clumsy enough to roll near a fence and cast himself by trapping his legs between the boards. Carefully free his legs and use the rope method described in tip 92 to roll him over. (photos.com)

tip 92.

If a horse does become cast, quickly find help. It takes at least two strong, horse-savvy adults to safely roll a horse back over. Find two long, soft cotton ropes (if you must use lead ropes, make sure they don't have stud chains). While your helper stays at the horse's head to keep him as calm as possible, tie the end of one rope around the horse's front pastern tightly enough that it won't slip, but not so tight that it might cut off circulation. Being very careful to stay out of kicking range, tie the second rope around his hind pastern. If he's lying on his left side, tie the ropes to his left legs. This is very important. Pulling on the top two legs will not give you enough leverage and may even cause injury to the horse.

Now, each person must take hold of a rope. If you have a third person to help, she should stay at the horse's head to guide it as he rolls over. On the count of three, both rope-holders pull steadily as hard as they can. Do *not* yank or jerk the ropes, which could cause rope burns or other injury to the pasterns. Unless the horse is very large or is resisting violently, two people should be able to roll the horse back to its other side. Then move out of kicking range as quickly as possible; the horse is likely to flail his legs as he struggles to his feet. Once he has settled enough for you to approach safely, remove the ropes.

tip 93.
While hauling, if you stop and must leave your truck and trailer unattended at a rest stop, even for a few minutes, always check your horses, doors, tires, brake plug, hitch, and safety chain before continuing on your trip. Some passersby may think it's funny to play practical jokes. Such "pranks" as unhitching a trailer are rare occurrences, but it's definitely better to be safe than sorry.

Of course, in the best-case scenario, you'll never leave your rig unattended at all. Ideally, you should haul with at least two people, so that someone is always able to stay with the horses while the other runs into the rest stop for coffee and snacks.

tip 94.

Even if you don't own a trailer, you should learn how to hook up, load, and drive a rig. In an emergency, there may not be a qualified driver available to haul your horse to the vet. Or if you are hauling with someone and you're traveling long distances, you'll be able to spell the driver. The more you know about hauling, the better passenger you can be. You'll be able to assist the driver and will have a second pair of knowledgeable eyes to spot potentially dangerous situations that may arise.

Streak and George are happy to stand in the trailer with bags of hay as a snack.

tip 95. Trailers can seem scary to a horse,

but with a little practice and patience, loading does not have to be a trial. If your horse requires half an hour, four people, a lunge line, a dressage whip, and a two-pound bag of carrots to get onto the trailer, consider this trick:

Hook up your trailer to the truck and park it on level ground near the barn. Stock it with hay and your horse's usual ration of grain. When dinnertime comes, load him (however you need to do it) and feed him his grain in the trailer. Don't drive anywhere. Just load him up, secure the butt bar and tie him, praise him, feed him, and unload. Do the same thing the following day. After several repetitions, he'll be practically dragging you to the trailer. At that point you can start practicing loading him during non-dinner hours and taking short, comfortable, slow drives around the neighborhood.

This tire needs air before the trailer goes anywhere.

tip 96. Every time you haul, perform the

following safety checks before loading the horses onto the trailer:

- Check the tread (minimum of ¼ inch), inflation, and condition of all truck and trailer tires and spare tires.

- Check that your first aid kit is complete.

- Make sure you have jacks, wheel chocks, and reflective safety triangles. The jacks should be capable of lifting the fully loaded trailer in case you have a flat tire in a place where unloading the horses is unsafe, such as the breakdown lane of a highway.

- Lift the mats and check floorboards for signs of rot or weakness.

- Check inside the trailer for any loose screws or any other sharp edges that may cut a horse.

- Check that all lights (marker, tail, brake, directional, and interior) are functioning.

- Check hitch welds, safety chain welds, and snaps.

- Grease hitch ball if needed.

- Test brakes.

A clean horse is a happy horse.

—Horseman's proverb

tip 97.

Don't touch that tail! If you want your horse's tail to be long, full, and luxurious, the best thing to do is *nothing*. Each time you comb or brush a tail, no matter how careful you are, you'll inevitably break off or pull out many of the hairs. It takes seven years for a tail hair to grow from the root to its full length; do you really want to wait that long?

Leave the tail alone until the day before a show. Then, wash it with horse shampoo and conditioner. As the tail is drying, apply a commercial detangler (my favorite is Cowboy Magic) and carefully separate each hair by hand—*not* with a brush or comb. This method is time-consuming but essential if you are to avoid unnecessary damage.

tip 98. Many owners let their horses'

manes grow long and shaggy during the winter months. Come spring, they are faced with an overgrown rat's nest to rip into shape with the pulling comb. This process can be painful and trying for even the most tolerant of equine beauty queens. To spare your horse's aching neck, not to mention your own blistered fingers, take the time to do some routine thinning during the winter. Pull manes at Christmas, on Valentine's Day, and on Easter. Then when show season rolls around, you'll have a lot less work to do. The best time to pull a mane is right after a ride or other exercise, when the horse's pores are open and the hair will pull out much more easily.

Bonus tip: If your horse is one of those that *hates* having its mane pulled, spray on an over-the-counter sore-throat spray (such as Chloraseptic) before you begin. The topical analgesics in the medicine will dull the nerve endings in his neck and make things much more pleasant for everyone—not to mention that lovely menthol aroma.

---

tip 99. Before you body-clip, bathe your

horse to remove the dirt, sweat, and oils that can clog and dull the clipper blades. After bathing, give him a final rinse with a fragrance-free liquid fabric softener to allow the clippers to glide smoothly through the coat and reduce the stripy appearance that clipping can produce. Before using any new product on a horse, however, be sure to test a small area and wait twenty-four hours before using it on his whole body. Check for any allergic reactions such as itching, redness and heat, flaking skin, or hives.

tip 100.

After bathing with shampoo, rinse with clean water and then do a final rinse of one cup of white vinegar per gallon of water. The vinegar will cut the soap residue and prevent it from leaving an itchy, coat-dulling film. It has the added benefit of repelling flies. Don't worry: there will be no vinegary smell once it dries. You can also wipe undiluted vinegar directly onto the coat as an inexpensive fly repellent.

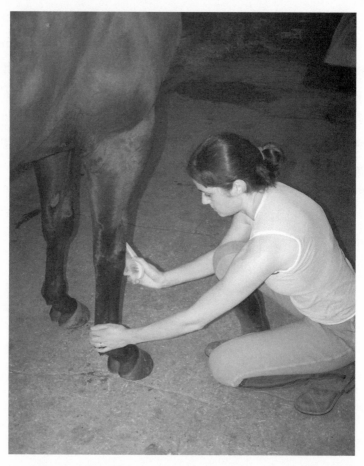

Grooming is the time you'll spot developing problems in your horse's body. Stay alert and pay attention to the details.

tip 101.

During your daily grooming session, run your hands over every inch of your horse, checking for lumps, bumps, nicks, scrapes, bites, kicks, bruises, splints, hoof chips or cracks, hives, ticks, scratches, swelling, itchy spots, hair loss, scabs, heat, flaking skin, runny nose, irritated eyes, dull coat, visible ribs, saddle sores, rub marks, girth galls, splinters, thorns, stone bruises, tender areas, attitude changes . . . you get the idea. The more careful you are, the earlier you will spot developing problems and the sooner you can take action to fix them.

Further Reading

Books

Equine Research, *The Horseman's Veterinary Encyclopedia* (Guilford, Connecticut: The Lyons Press, 2005)

Fry, Joan, *Backyard Horsekeeping* (Guilford, Connecticut: The Lyons Press, 2004)

Hill, Cherry, *Horsekeeping on a Small Acreage, 2nd Ed.* (North Adams, Massachusetts: Storey Publishing, 2005)

Price, Steven D. et al., *The Whole Horse Catalog* (Fireside/Simon & Schuster, 1978, revised 1998)

Magazines

Equus and *Practical Horseman*
Primedia Equine Network
656 Quince Orchard Road
Suite 600
Gaithersburg, MD 20878
www.equisearch.com

Western Horseman
3850 N. Nevada Ave.
Colorado Springs, CO 80907-5339
www.westernhorseman.com

Websites

www.chronicleforums.com

The *Chronicle of the Horse* bulletin board forums are a place where horse people of various disciplines meet to discuss topics of mutual concern.

www.horsecity.com

HorseCity is an excellent source for all kinds of horse-related information, from tack and training to health and safety.

www.equisearch.com

EquiSearch is the Web site portal for *Practical Horseman* and *Equus* magazines, among others.

Acknowledgments

This book represents the combined knowledge and expertise of the many capable horsemen and women I've worked with throughout my life. Credit goes to all of them.

In particular, I thank Mott Atherholt and Caroline Dowd for giving me my start in the horse world and for teaching me from the very beginning to be a good horseperson as well as a rider. Thanks also to Jennifer and Rob Sisk at Crystal Wood Stables in Durham, Connecticut; and Marty Whittle at Top Cat Farm in Killingworth, Connecticut, for generously allowing me to photograph their beautiful and well-kept facilities. At the Sisks' and at Marty's farms, the horses always come first.

And thanks to Suzanne Mancheski for being a model and to Maggie and Kim Peterson, Elizabeth Marks, and Julie Gladstone for photos of Jim, Jaguar, and Alfie.

This book would also not have come to be without the support and faith of the wonderful people at The Lyons Press. Thanks very much to Steve Price, my intrepid editor and mentor, for wisdom and equanimity, and to Jay Cassell for taking a chance on me. Thanks to

Chris Mongillo, Sheryl Kober, and Kirsten Livingston for going the extra mile for the design, and to Cynthia Goss for copyediting and kind words.

Thanks, of course, to my parents, and especially to my husband Jason for his support, patience, and skill with a camera.